NATIONAL GEOGRAPHIC KiDS

DOG SCIENCE UNLEASHED

FUN ACTIVITIES TO DO WITH YOUR CANINE COMPANION

JODI WHEELER-TOPPEN

PHOTOGRAPHS BY MATTHEW RAKOLA

NATIONAL GEOGRAPHIC
WASHINGTON, D.C.

CONTENTS

SNIFFING OUT SENSES

FIT FIDO

CLEVER CANINES

PAMPERED POOCHES

INTRODUCTION

You already know so much about your canine companion—his favorite treat, his best tricks, even his all-time favorite snuggle spot. But what's going on in his mind when he's drooling for a scrumptious snack? How fast is his heart beating when he's curled up, tired after a *ruff* day of play? What's he thinking when he looks up at you?

Get ready to find out! You'll discover tons of amazing canine science on every page of this book. Complete the hands-on activities to explore the science behind your dog's senses, how your pup is built to move, how your dog learns, and so much more. Whether you have a tiny terrier or a massive mastiff, there is so much that you and your furry friend can learn together.

Some of the science in this book will be the same for all dogs, no matter what breed you have. Other activities are designed to help you understand the most important pooch on Earth: your own. You can bet there's not a dog on Earth with exactly the same lovable combination of nuzzling nose, drippy drool, perfect paws, and tail-wagging spunk.

So, let out a happy howl and get ready to unleash some doggone good science with the most faithful lab partner you'll ever find—your dog!

⚠ SAFETY GUIDELINES AND TIPS

Dear Parents,

Each page in this book has been designed to actively engage your child in fun, creative, and challenging ways. While we recommend that your young scientist have adult supervision for ALL of the projects in this book, certain activities REQUIRE adult supervision and SHOULD NOT be conducted UNLESS an ADULT is actively involved. We have flagged those activities with red labels that say "Grab a Grown-up."

Before you begin an activity, please read and discuss the following SAFETY GUIDELINES with your child:

🐾 Be careful during the activities, and use extra caution when working with tools such as sharp knives, scissors, or hot objects.

🐾 Prepare yourself to work in a safe manner (e.g., heat resistant mitts when working with hot objects).

🐾 Create a safe work space (e.g., a fenced-in yard).

🐾 Use safety equipment (e.g., have a fire-response tool nearby when working with heat, have a first aid kit in the house).

🐾 Wash and dry your hands before and after each activity.

🐾 Follow the directions for each activity and take your time.

🐾 Read and follow the safety tips on applicable activities, the guidelines on all product labels, and use your own common sense and judgment.

⚠ DOG SAFETY

The activities in this book are designed to be fun for both kids and their pets. Just like humans, dogs enjoy new challenges! Please review these guidelines with your child to make sure any participating pup is safe, comfortable, and having fun.

🐾 Only do these activities with a dog that knows your child well and is comfortable around your child.

🐾 Watch for signs that the dog is unhappy. If any of these activities seem to make the dog uncomfortable or upset, stop immediately.

🐾 Even a dog that is enjoying an activity needs a break. Make sure the dog has access to water throughout these activities and if he wants to stop, let him.

🐾 If your dog is on a special diet, check with his veterinarian before feeding him treats. Always check with the dog's owner before feeding him anything.

🐾 Clean up when you are done, so your pooch doesn't accidentally eat any leftover materials.

🐾 If you decide to alter an activity or try a new version, make sure the new plan is safe for both your child and the dog.

HOW TO USE THIS BOOK

S cience experiments are often worked out through trial and error, and dogs can be unpredictable. Put the two together, and you're in for a wild ride. Because dogs come in so many shapes, sizes, and personalities, not every activity will work with every pup. Some may work better than others, and others may not work at all. Don't be discouraged—you're in good company! Even the dog scientists interviewed in this book had challenges making their experiments work. Alexandra Horowitz (see page 58) tried several experimental designs before creating her "mirror" test for dogs, and Cherie Pucheu-Haston (see page 74) is still figuring out how to simplify the process of diagnosing food allergies in dogs.

If your dog (aka lab partner) isn't eager to try something the way it is described, find a method she likes better. For example, if she's skittish of the scent containers used in "Awesome Odors" on page 18, she might like to smell scents that have been rubbed on the sidewalk. On the other hand, if you find an activity that she seems to enjoy, stay with it! Some activities give suggestions for going further, but you can always brainstorm new ideas to expand on any of the experiments. The possibilities are endless. Just remember to give your pup a break and reward her with positive reinforcement, such as tasty treats, belly rubs, and, of course, telling her what a great dog she is!

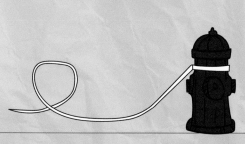

HALF BATH

FIND OUT IF SHAMPOO IS RIGHT FOR YOUR PUP

> **Difficulty Level:**
> **Grab a Grown-**

> **Active Time Need**
> **20 minutes init**
> **then 10 minute**
> **for 4 weeks**

I f you wore a coat all the time, eventually it would have to be washed. What about your furry friend? Experts disagree on how frequently a dog needs washing. Try shampooing just one side of your dog to figure out the ideal washing schedule for your pooch.

YOU NEED

hose or bathtub with cup
 for pouring
shampoo made specifically
 for dogs
towels

TIP
Make sure you pick a shampoo for pooches. A dog's skin is less acidic than human skin, so human shampoo can cause irritation.

Even a simple activity can have tricky bits. Our young scientists and their pups helped find the *ruff* spots and found ways to make things go more smoothly.

Need a friend or a grown-up? Sometimes an extra pair of hands and eyes comes in handy, and this box will tell you if you need them. Of course, a friend can always make things more fun, and be a source of great new ideas, but you and your pup can do many of these experiments with just the two of you.

1

2

3

4

RATING SCALE

ODOR:
1. PLEASANT AROMA. I'D USE HIM AS A PILLOW.
2. SMELLS LIKE A DOG, BUT NOT IN A BAD WAY.
3. STARTING TO GET A LITTLE STINKY. I WOULDN'T WANT HIM ON MY BED.
4. P.U.! THIS DOG REEKS. IT'S A BATH EMERGENCY!

DIRT AND OIL:
1. LOOKS CLEAN AND FEELS SOFT.
2. LOOKS CLEAN, BUT LEAVES A LITTLE ICKY FEELING ON MY HANDS WHEN I PET HIM.
3. DIRT SHOWS IN A FEW PLACES.
4. GOOD GRIEF! DON'T EVEN COME IN THE HOUSE LIKE THAT!

7 In four weeks, analyze your data. If the side without shampoo stayed fresh and clean, or was less likely to need a scratch, rinsing and brushing may be all he needs. On the other hand, if the side with shampoo stayed in better shape, a good soap and scrub may be the way to go.

INSTRUCTIONS

1 Begin by wetting your dog thoroughly. You may need to rub his fur with your fingers to help the water soak in.

2 Decide which side of his body you want to shampoo. To make it fair, pick the left or right side, not the front or back, as dogs do very different things with their hind ends than their front. Remember which side you picked!

3 Pretend there is a line running down the center of your dog's back, from his nose to his tail. Carefully shampoo your dog on the side you selected. Be sure to get his back, legs, paws, and belly on this side. Avoid his head if you aren't sure you can keep the shampoo out of his eyes and ears.

4 Thoroughly rinse the shampoo, so none of it is left to irritate his skin.

5 Towel him dry.

6 Check out his cleanliness over the next four weeks. Twice a week, use the rating scales on this page to evaluate his odor and dirt levels. Jot down which side he scratches each time you observe it.

TAKE IT FURTHER
Try comparing two different shampoos by washing one side with one shampoo and one with the other. Does it matter which brand you buy?

TO BATHE OR NOT TO BATHE
Some dog experts believe that too many baths are bad for a dog's skin. They argue that the oils in his fur are natural and removing them can irritate his skin and make him more likely to stink. Other experts believe that bathing regularly, with the right sort of shampoo, is exactly what a pooch needs to stay clean, healthy, and fresh-smelling. In all likelihood, there is truth in both positions. Some dogs probably keep their coats naturally neat. Others have a knack for finding the nastiest place in the yard to go for a roll.

Some of these experiments were just begging for more exploration. Some of our ideas and questions are listed. You can come up with more!

PAMPERED POOCHES **69**

MEET OUR SCIENTISTS AND DOGS

Fiona, 12 & Daisy, 4

Ariana, 13 & Scarlett, 1

Gabriel, 15 & Peace, 3

Elsie, 7 & Diesel, 11

Henry, 14 & Maisy, 7

Emilee, 17 & Milou, 1

Jordan, 15 & Pepper, 5

Karisa, 17, Emily, 14, Sofia, 15 & Lily, 4

Natalie, 10 & Daisy, 9

Noah, 12 & Emmie, 6

Lilly, 14 & Chloe, 2

Luke, 13 & Buddy, 11

Sayla, 14 & Max, 7

Tara, 15 & Buddha, 7

Madeline, 13 & Daisy, 5

OFF TO THE RACES

SET UP A FAIR EXPERIMENT

> Difficulty Level:
> **Medium**

> Active Time Needed:
> **15 minutes**

Who's faster—you or your pup? There's only one way to find out: a race! But it's got to be set up fair and square to give you both a chance to show your speed. You'll want to start at the same place and time, run the same distance, and both sprint across the same patch of ground. Otherwise, one of you will have an advantage. Think carefully as you set up this contest, because—believe it or not—you'll also be practicing science!

YOU NEED

a friend
safe, fenced-in area where your dog
   can run free
leash
treats
marker for the starting and finish lines

TIP
Set the treat on a box or upside-down bowl to make it easy for Fido to see where he's headed.

1

4

5

INSTRUCTIONS

1 Find a place to race with your dog. Decide on a starting line and a finish line.

2 Put your dog on a leash. Show your dog a treat and place it at the finish line.

3 Walk your dog to the starting line. Give him to your friend, and get ready to run!

4 Have your friend yell "Go" and release your dog.

5 Run as fast as you can to the finish line.

FAIR IS FAIR Science experiments can be like a race. When scientists are making comparisons, they make sure that everything is exactly the same between the situations they are comparing, except for the one thing they want to test. Just like you can't know who's really fastest if your race isn't fair, scientists can't know if the results of their experiments are sound if they change more than one thing at a time. Some of the activities in this book will uncover your dog's unique preferences. For example, in chapter 1 you'll get the scoop on your dog's favorite treat. To keep it fair, you'll want to serve all the treats in the same kind of bowl. Otherwise, you can't be sure if he likes the new treat best or is intrigued by the new bowl! You will get the best results from the experiments in this book if you think about making each one a fair test.

SNIFFING OUT SENSES

HOW YOUR DOG SEES THE WORLD

If a friend asked you to describe your room, you might tell him what posters you have on your walls, the color of your bedspread, or where you have your furniture. In short, you would probably describe what you see.

But what if your dog were answering the question? He might say that your scent wafts comfortingly off the bed, that the dirty clothes in your laundry basket smell amazing, and that the trash can is a fountain of enticing odors! From there, your dog might mention the high-pitched whine of your digital clock that you don't hear, the feeling of your bookshelf against his wagging tail, and the nice tasty spot under your desk that he likes to lick and lick and lick. As for vision, he may not have much to report—dogs experience the world very differently from humans.

Round up your pup partner, and get ready to find out how the world smells, feels, looks, tastes, and sounds to your dog.

EXPLORE!
FIDO'S FIVE SENSES

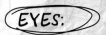

EYES:

Your dog doesn't see as many colors or as much detail as you do, but his eyes are perfectly adapted to see movement. He has wide pupils to capture lots of light, and motion-detecting cells across the back of his eye. One researcher worked with a dog that could recognize his owner from a mile away, but only if his owner was moving!

Whether your dog has a nose for adventure or just the crumbs in the couch cushions, that cute furry face is ready to sense the world around him.

Each of a dog's sense organs—his nose, tongue, ears, eyes, and skin—contains special nerve cells that get the scoop on what's around. But a sense organ by itself can't figure out much. It has to send intel to the brain to find out what it means. The brain compares the sensory information to the dog's previous experiences, looking for a match. Is that the sound of food hitting the bowl? Woof!

Does your dog dive for cover when the vacuum cleaner comes out? She's probably hearing irritating, high-pitched sounds that you can't hear.

EARS:

You might think that dogs' ears are just for listening for the crinkle of the treat bag. But in fact, long, droopy ears also help some dogs ... smell. The trailing ears on bloodhounds and basset hounds stir up smells from the ground and hold them in place until the nose kicks in. But what if your dog has pricked ears that stand up on his head? They may not do much for scent, but unlike floppy-eared dogs, those with pricked ears can turn them from side to side to locate important sounds.

NOSE:

When it comes to smell, dogs leave us in the dust. Fido's super sniffer is lined with scent detectors that can pick up the tiniest traces of odor. You might catch a whiff of body odor from across the room when your brother comes in from basketball practice. But your dog could smell him from across a football field!

VIBRISSAE:

These are long, stiff hairs that sense movement around your dog's face. They are anchored deep in your dog's skin and surrounded by nerve cells. Since the **vibrissae** are stiff, the nerves can feel even light breezes. Dogs have trouble seeing detail up close, so they sweep the area around them with their vibrissae to feel for details in their environment.

Vibrissae are especially important to dogs who can't see. They use them to keep from bumping into furniture.

TONGUE:

Taste just isn't your dog's priority. It's the one sense where humans outdo dogs. You have around 9,000 taste buds. Your dog tastes with just 1,700.

BELGIAN MALINOIS POLICE DOG

THE NOSE KNOWS. OR DOES IT?

Your super sniffer has the ability to detect even faint odors. But without training, she doesn't know which smells are important to you or how to let you know when she smells them. People put dogs to work sniffing out drugs, bombs, or missing persons, but the dogs have to be taught which scents matter and how to alert their owners to the smell.

AWESOME ODORS

FIND YOUR DOG'S FAVORITE SMELL

> **Difficulty Level:**
> **Grab a Grown-up**

> **Active Time Needed:**
> **30 minutes**

It's no secret that dogs like smells that make people say "Pee-ew!" Your pup may love to find the stinkiest corner of the yard and roll, roll, roll. Or he may get into the garbage and spread the stench high and low.

When those icky odor chemicals enter your dog's nose, they travel through the air until they smack into a smell **receptor.** That receptor notifies the brain, and the brain tries to recognize the smell—like a matching game. Humans have about five million smell receptors, but dogs have up to 300 million! Try this activity to find some smells that will make those receptors happy.

TAKE IT FURTHER

Now that you know your pup's new favorite smell, use it to spice up his time outside. Rub the scent on a rag and hide it in your yard. Use bits of scented material to make a trail leading to the rag. Does he follow the trail to the rag?

SUPER SNIFFER When a dog gets a whiff of something new, he sniffs the odor into an amazing smelling machine. His nose has a special pocket called the **olfactory recess** that is separated from the rest of his nose by a thin bone. He can store air in that recess while he continues to breathe in and out normally, which gives his brain more time to interpret the smell.

And if he wants more of that same smell? Take a close look at his nose. He has two big nostrils with slits along the sides. Air goes in the round section and out through the slits. This way, the exhaled air doesn't get in the way of the incoming smells.

NOSTRILS
Your dog breathes in air through his round nostrils.

SLITS
Air is exhaled through the slits on the side.

WORCESTERSHIRE

TIP
If you stack the lids, you can punch several of them at a time.

1

GINGER

LEMON JUICE

2

YOU NEED

hammer and nail
4 identical plastic containers with lids
4 unusual odors (some ideas: mint mouthwash, Worcestershire sauce, ginger or another strong spice, dirty sock, or toy that a friend's dog has used)

INSTRUCTIONS

1 Ask an adult to help you use the hammer and nail to punch 10 holes in the top of each plastic container.

2 Place some of each scent into its own separate plastic container and put the lid on it. Shake to get the smell circulating.

3 With your dog out of the room, place the containers in a row with a few inches between them.

4 Let your dog into the room. Record how long he spends with each container over one minute. He will spend the most time with the scent that is most interesting to him.

MOUTHWASH

LEMON JUICE

GIN[GER]

4

⚠ SAFETY NOTE
Do not leave your dog alone with the plastic containers. You wouldn't want him to get so interested in a smell that he eats the plastic!

TASTE TEST

DISCOVER YOUR DOG'S FAVORITE FLAVORS

> Difficulty Level:
> **Medium**

> Active Time Needed:
> **30 minutes**

It's a bit tricky to figure out a dog's favorite flavors. They tend to be "eat first, ask questions later" animals. Spreading treats out on the ground can slow them down and give them time to pick out the bites they like best. Use this technique to find the flavors your pup prefers.

YOU NEED

painter's tape
yardstick or meterstick
plain bite-size dog biscuits (store-bought or from recipe on p. 22)
¼ cup (59 mL) beef or chicken broth
¼ cup (59 mL) lemon juice
juice from a can of tuna packed in water
9 shallow bowls
pencil and paper

1

2

TIP
Leave the yardstick on one side to mark the top of your grid to help you remember the order of your flavored treats.

TAKE IT FURTHER

Repeat the activity on another day to see if your dog always hankers for the same snacks. Or change out the flavors: Try peanut butter, peppermint tea, or Worcestershire sauce. Try healthy snacks. Would she choose a carrot chunk, some sweet potato, or an apple slice?

INSTRUCTIONS

1 Prepare the grid. Use the painter's tape and yardstick to create a three-by-three-foot (or one-by-one-meter) square in a clear area. Use more tape to divide the square into nine boxes, each about a foot (or 33 cm) wide.

2 Prepare the treats. Dip three treats into the beef broth, three into the lemon juice, and three into the tuna juice.

3 Place one treat in each square on your grid. Make sure to mix it up: Don't put all of the same kind of treats next to each other.

4 Draw the grid on your piece of paper and write down what you put in each square.

5 Release your dog in front of the grid. Use your paper to record the order in which she eats the treats.

6 When she finishes, list the treats she selected from start to finish. Did she choose some treats over others? Were there any she wouldn't eat at all?

SAFETY NOTE

⚠ Make sure that whatever you give her is safe for dogs to eat, and don't offer too many things in one day. You don't want to ruin her dinner!

GULP! Under all the slobber, your dog's tongue is coated with taste buds. If all goes well, **molecules** of flavor dissolve in the spit and seep into the taste buds, where sensory cells recognize the taste. Most dogs like meat flavors and sweets, and dislike sour foods. But this assumes the object stays in the mouth long enough to be tasted—some dogs gobble their food so quickly that it doesn't even register with their taste buds. Fortunately, a dog's stomach acid is 10 times stronger than a human's, so if Rover gulps something rotten, the acid will kill the bacteria. Unfortunately, a gulp-y dog can still get into trouble. Veterinarians remove all kinds of things that have gotten stuck in a dog's stomach. One Great Dane swallowed 43½ socks!

DELICIOUS DOG TREATS

BAKE SOMETHING SPECIAL FOR YOUR PUP

> Difficulty Level:
> **Grab a Grown-up**

> Active Time Needed:
> **15 minutes to prepare,
> 20 minutes to bake**

All this research can make a dog hungry. Cook up some dog treats to show her what a good dog she is!

YOU NEED

1 cup (125 g) flour
½ cup (45 g) quick-cooking oats
1 large egg
¼ cup plus 2 tablespoons (89 mL) water
mixing bowl
rolling pin
cookie cutters
baking sheet or pan
aluminum foil or cooking spray
cutting board

In the United States, dog owners spend about three billion dollars on dog treats each year.

INSTRUCTIONS

1 Preheat the oven to 400°F (200°C).

2 Mix all ingredients in a large bowl. Knead the dough with your fingers to finish the mixing.

3 Lightly flour the cutting board and rolling pin. Roll the dough on the cutting board until it is about a quarter-inch (6 mm) thick.

4 Use cookie cutters to create individual treats.

5 Cover the baking sheet with aluminum foil or cooking spray. Place the treats on the baking sheet.

6 Have an adult help you bake the cookies for 16–20 minutes, or until the edges brown. Allow them to cool completely before offering them to your dog.

TAIL-WAGGING TREATS

THIS RECIPE IS INTENTIONALLY BLAND, SO THAT IT CAN BE COMBINED WITH VARIOUS FLAVORS FOR TASTE-TESTING. TO TURN THESE INTO TREATS YOUR DOG WILL BEG FOR, PUT IN ⅓ CUP OF SOMETHING OFF THIS LIST INSTEAD OF THE EGG:

🐾 PEANUT BUTTER
🐾 CHICKEN BROTH
🐾 BEEF BABY FOOD
🐾 CANNED PUMPKIN
🐾 PLAIN YOGURT

6

HIDDEN IN PLAIN SIGHT

DISCOVER HOW YOUR DOG SEES COLOR

> Difficulty Level:
> **Medium**

> Active Time Needed:
> **20 minutes**

TIP
If your dog isn't a big fan of fetch, try using red and blue treat holders or rubbing a bit of peanut butter on each ball.

A dog's eye is an amazing information collector. In just one glance, it picks up light, shape, color, and movement. The back of her eye has two types of cells for taking it all in. **Rod cells** are extremely sensitive to shades of light, and they can detect light and motion even in very dark places. **Cone cells** recognize color.

Take your dog out to a grassy field for a game of fetch and an eye test to put those cells to work. Which is easier for her to see: a red ball or a blue one? Figure it out by timing how long it takes your dog to find each one.

YOU NEED

red ball
blue ball
stopwatch or timer
green, grassy field or yard

1

5

3

3 Start timing as soon as you release her. Record how long it takes her to find the ball.

4 If your dog does not find the ball within 30 seconds, then fetch the ball yourself and record it as "gave up."

5 Repeat the procedure with the red ball. Throw it about the same distance, but to a slightly different location.

6 Continue until you have at least five throws with each ball. Vary the location with each throw, and make sure it lands in a grassy area each time.

7 Figure out the average time that it took your dog to find each color. To do this, add up the total time she spent looking for the blue ball. Count any tries that you marked "gave up" as 30 seconds. Divide this total by five. Repeat for the red ball. What color was easier for her to find?

INSTRUCTIONS

1 Hold your dog or keep her on a leash. Show her the blue ball and throw it.

2 Once the ball has landed, release her to find the ball. (If she is loose when you throw the ball, she will follow it to where it lands instead of looking for it.)

WHAT A HUMAN SEES

WHAT A DOG SEES

WHAT DOGS CAN'T SEE

Finally, a sense where humans outrank dogs! Humans have three kinds of cone cells to detect color. One senses purple and blue light, one responds most strongly to green, and one picks up a range from green to red. Dogs have only two types of cone cells. One is similar to our purple/blue cones. The other picks up light that is yellowish green. To a dog, red ends up looking very similar to green. So a red ball lying in green grass is camouflaged!

WHAT SPOT SEES

TEST YOUR DOG'S FIELD OF VISION

> Difficulty Level:
> **Medium**

> Active Time Needed:
> **15 minutes**

You're on a walk and your dog goes bananas—there's a squirrel off to your left! But how did he even see it over there? He may be able to see farther back than you would expect. Some dogs have a very large field of vision. Find out if your dog can see farther around than you.

YOU NEED

a helpful friend
a dog treat
painter's tape

INSTRUCTIONS

1 Use painter's tape to make a straight line on the floor.

2 Have your dog stand or sit on the line.

3 Have a friend stand in front of your dog holding the treat to keep your dog looking forward. Crouch down about four feet (1.2 m) to the side of your dog.

4 Look for his pupil—the dark spot in the middle of his eye. Back up until you reach the last point where you can see his pupil. Use the tape to mark where you are. Give your dog the treat!

5 Repeat the procedure to find your own field of vision. Sit in the same place your dog sat and stare straight ahead. Ask your friend to mark the last place she can see your pupil. Who can see farther behind: you or your dog?

TIP
If your dog keeps trying to grab the treat instead of sitting, have your friend hold the treat on the other side of a glass door or window.

2

4

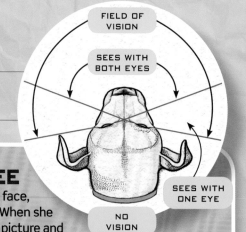

FIELD OF VISION

SEES WITH BOTH EYES

SEES WITH ONE EYE

NO VISION

WHAT DOGS CAN SEE

If your dog has a short nose and a flat face, her eyes are probably close together. When she looks forward, both eyes see a similar picture and send it to the brain. Her brain overlaps the pictures and creates a 3-D image. However, in dogs with long noses and narrow faces, the images that the eyes send to the brain don't overlap as much. These dogs don't have as much depth perception, but have a wider field of vision.

WHISTLE FOR WILLIE

WHAT YOUR DOG HEARS

> Difficulty Level:
> **Medium**

> Active Time Needed:
> **30 minutes**

Tweet, tweet! The whistle squeals. Your breath makes the whistle vibrate and bump into air molecules nearby. Those molecules bump into neighboring molecules, which bump into more molecules, which bump into more … you get the picture. The sound travels through the air as a wave. When the wave hits Spot's eardrum, he hears the sound—if his ear and brain are tuned to recognize it. What sounds make the biggest impression on your dog? Make two straw whistles to find out.

YOU NEED

2 plastic straws
scissors
ruler

INSTRUCTIONS

1 Measure a half inch (13 mm) from the end of one straw. Flatten that section of the straw by pressing it against a hard surface.

2 Trim the edges of the flat portion of the straw to create a triangular mouthpiece.

3 Play the straw whistle by holding it between your lips where the mouthpiece meets the rest of the straw. Blow.

4 Repeat the process with a second straw, but trim the end so that the entire whistle (mouthpiece and all) is only about three inches (8 cm) long.

5 When your dog is resting but awake, stand nearby and blow the long whistle. Note your dog's reaction.

6 Allow him to settle back down. Blow the short whistle and note his reaction.

7 Repeat each whistle several times to see if there is a pattern in your dog's responses.

⚠ SAFETY NOTE
If the sound from either whistle seems to make your dog uncomfortable, stop blowing.

THAT HERTZ!

Did you notice that the longer whistle produced a lower pitch than the shorter whistle? Pitch depends on how fast an object vibrates. Scientists measure pitch by counting the number of vibrations in a second, a unit known as **hertz (Hz).** The lowest key on a piano, for example is 27.5 Hz, or 27.5 vibrations per second. Most sounds, like your whistles, are a mixture of pitches. Most dogs will at least glance your way when you blow either whistle to see what you are up to. However, they usually respond more strongly to the shorter, high-pitched whistle. They may look up sharply and focus their ears, or get up and come over to investigate the source of the sound.

in the LAB

A PICTURE IS WORTH A THOUSAND SCENTS

The dog's nose is a remarkable odor collector, but the real work of smelling takes place in the brain. Just like in humans, a dog's brain sorts the odors inhaled through the nose and figures out what they mean. But what happens inside a dog's marvelous mind when taking a big sniff? Gregory Berns, a scientist at Emory University in Atlanta, Georgia, U.S.A., has found a way to watch the brain smell.

Berns uses a special device called a magnetic resonance imaging (MRI) machine to take a picture that shows where blood is flowing in the brain. In all animals, more blood goes to areas that are doing work—whether those are the muscles, the organs, or even the brain. So when Berns uses an MRI machine on a sniffing dog, he can see which parts of the brain are active.

Dogs have an extra organ for smelling that humans don't have. Called the **vomeronasal organ,** it is found at the back of the nose and is especially sensitive to the sort of molecules found in sweat.

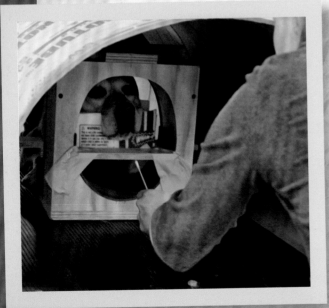

PEEK INTO THE BRAIN

A yellow Labrador retriever named Kady trots into the lab and sits calmly while Berns places earplugs in her ears and wraps her head with gauze to keep them in place. MRI machines are noisy, so Berns is careful to protect Kady's hearing. Kady walks up a ramp into the MRI, lies down, and places her head on a specially made headrest. She stays very still, just as she has been trained to do. Berns turns on the MRI and begins the procedure.

In this study, Berns has Kady sniff gauze pads with different odors. One gauze pad had spent time in her owner's armpit and carried his smell. One had been rubbed on a dog that Kady knew. A third came from a person Kady did not know, and the fourth from a dog she had never met. The final odor was Kady herself. Berns repeated the same process with 11 other dogs.

A WHIFF OF HOME

When he examined the MRI results, Berns could see that the area of the brain that processes smells was activated by all five odors. But another area was activated when the dogs smelled the odor of their own human. Extra blood went to a section of the brain that usually is active when an animal gets a reward. This suggests that even when you aren't around, your smell may be enough to make your dog think of good things.

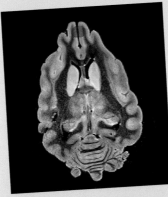

MRI MACHINES TAKE A PICTURE OF THE BLOOD FLOW IN THE BRAIN. IN THESE IMAGES, THE RED AREAS OF THE BRAIN ARE ACTIVATED WHEN THE DOG IS SMELLING SOMETHING, AND THE YELLOW PARTS WHEN SHE'S FEELING REWARDED.

The Labrador retriever is the most popular dog breed in the United States. These friendly dogs learn quickly and happily lend a paw to research.

CHAPTER 2

FIT FIDO

THE SCIENCE BEHIND YOUR HEALTHY HOUND

Some dogs dig diggin'. Some like to run and roll. Others love to chase or chew! Whatever his preference, your pup has a body that's made to move.

When you and your dog head out on a walk, some things are the same. You both have muscles that squeeze and pull on your bones. You both have a heart to pump blood to your muscles. You both breathe in oxygen and release carbon dioxide. But your pup does have some unique moves. He has four legs to coordinate when he runs and no way to grab a glass of water when all that exercise makes him hot and thirsty.

So grab a leash and get ready for fun ... but whatever you do, don't say "walk" until it's time to head out the door!

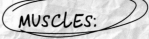

EXPLORE!
MUTTS IN MOTION

MUSCLES:

The back legs have the most powerful muscles in her body.

You know what gets your dog ready to romp—his favorite toy, a tossed stick, or the desire to smear a wet, sloppy kiss across your face. No matter what gets him moving, all of his body systems work together to keep him on the go.

BALANCING ACT

Dogs need their tails for more than just enthusiastically welcoming you home. If you run your hand along your dog's back, you'll feel a line of bumpy bones, called vertebrae. Together, these bones make up your dog's spine and tail. If his tail were made of one long bone, it wouldn't be able to bend. Luckily, your pup has around 22 vertebrae in his tail, depending on his breed. So his tail is flexible enough to move in all different directions. You might notice he uses it to balance while jumping or while crossing something narrow. His tail serves as a counterweight, the way a tightrope walker shifts his pole as he wobbles on the line.

Pups with leg problems can have wheelchairs! Roo, a Chihuahua-mix from Colorado, U.S.A., was born with no front legs. Her doctors fixed up a tiny cart to support her chest while she pushes her way around with her back legs.

BRAIN:

It signals the muscles to move, move, move.

TONGUE:

It's not just for tasting. She needs it to drink, as well!

HEART AND LUNGS:

A dog's heart and lungs send oxygen to all the muscles in her body. Her muscles need oxygen to contract.

The greyhound is the fastest dog breed, and Shakey Jakey might be the fastest greyhound. He ran a 1,706-foot (520-m) race in just 29.07 seconds. That's more than 40 miles an hour (64 km/h)!

ELBOW:

A dog's legs have the same basic bone structure as a human's arms and legs, but the bones are different lengths. This means that your dog's elbow is close to her body, and her back ankle is about where you might expect to find her knee.

BOUNTIFUL BLOOD

CALCULATE HOW MUCH BLOOD IS FLOWING THROUGH YOUR PUP

> **Difficulty Level:**
> **Easy**

> **Active Time Needed:**
> **5 minutes**

How much blood is pumping through your pup? You can do a quick calculation to find out! Blood volume depends on weight, so your first task is to lure Fido onto a scale. Scooping him up and holding him is the easiest approach. If your pooch weighs too much to lift, your vet or a parent likely has a record of the last time your pup was weighed.

YOU NEED

bathroom scale
measuring cup
pencil and paper

SOME TO SPARE

Don't panic if your dog gets a cut. All animals have a little more blood than they need. If you have a big dog, he can donate that extra volume to a blood bank—to learn more, see page 44. After he gives, his body will generate new blood cells to replace what was taken.

1

INSTRUCTIONS

1 Pick up your dog and step on the scale. Jot down how much you and your dog weigh together.

2 Put your dog down and weigh yourself. Jot down your weight.

3 Use those numbers to calculate your dog's weight using this formula: your weight when you are holding your dog – your weight all by yourself = your dog's weight.

4 A dog has about 34 milliliters (mL) of blood per pound (75 mL/kg). So if your dog weighs 25 pounds (11 kg), he will have about 850 mL of blood, or a little over 3½ cups. You can multiply your dog's weight by 34 mL or use the table here for an estimate.

5 Once you know your dog's blood volume, head for the kitchen and fill a measuring cup to get a look at how much liquid that is.

WEIGHT (LB)	ML	CUPS
10 (4.5 KG)	340	1⅓
20 (9.1 KG)	680	2¾
30 (13.6 KG)	1,020	4⅓
40 (18.1 KG)	1,360	5¾
50 (22.7 KG)	1,700	7¼
60 (27.2 KG)	2,040	8⅔
70 (31.8 KG)	2,380	10
80 (36.3 KG)	2,720	11½
90 (40.8 KG)	3,060	13
100 (45.4 KG)	3,400	14⅓

HEARTY HOUNDS

RECORD YOUR DOG'S HEART RATE

> Difficulty Level:
> **Easy**

> Active Time Needed:
> **5 minutes**

TIP
You may need to slide the stethoscope around until you find the heartbeat. It helps to work in a quiet space.

You head in for a checkup. Your doctor tells you to hop up on the table so she can listen to your heart and take your pulse. Your dog's checkup starts the same way. Veterinarians count the number of times a dog's heart beats in one minute, which is called the **heart rate.** But why should veterinarians have all the fun? Find your hound's resting heart rate using the instructions below.

YOU NEED

stethoscope (or make your own; see page 36)
clock or timer

SLOW AND STEADY

Don't expect a massive mutt to have a heart rate to match. Big dogs have lower heart rates than small dogs. The blood in a bulldog travels a long way before it needs another push, but it doesn't take long for the blood to flow through a tiny terrier. The resting heart rate for a seven-pound (3-kg) Yorkie might be 180 beats per minute, while an 80-pound (36-kg) Lab may have a heart rate closer to 80 beats per minute.

INSTRUCTIONS

1 Pick a time when your dog has been lying down for several minutes.

2 Gently rest the funnel end of your homemade stethoscope or the round flat bottom of a real stethoscope against the left side of your dog's chest, just behind his elbow, as shown in the picture.

3 Lean your ear against the other end of the cardboard tube or listen closely in the earbuds. If you don't hear a heartbeat, slowly shift your stethoscope around until you find it.

4 Count the number of beats that you hear in 15 seconds.

5 Multiply that number by four to get the number of beats per minute. This is your dog's resting heart rate.

HOMEMADE STETHOSCOPE

MAKE A TOOL TO HEAR YOUR HOUND'S HEART

> **Difficulty Level:**
> **Easy**

> **Active Time Needed:**
> **5 minutes**

The earliest stethoscopes were just tubes with a funnel-shaped end. The devices helped isolate the sound of the heart and lungs from the surrounding noise. You can make your own stethoscope with stuff you probably already have around the house.

YOU NEED

empty paper towel tube
small funnel (3 inches [7.6 cm] across or smaller)
packing or masking tape

2

INSTRUCTIONS

1 Insert the funnel into the paper towel tube.

2 Tape the funnel firmly in place by wrapping tape around the outside of the tube.

3 Place your ear against the paper towel tube and the funnel against the dog.

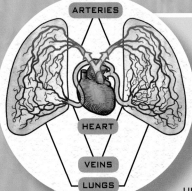

ARTERIES

HEART

VEINS

LUNGS

FROM THE HEART

Whoosh! Bandit's heart fills with blood. *Sploosh!* His heart squeezes. Out goes the blood, into the blood vessels. Blood from the right side of the heart heads to the lungs, where it picks up oxygen. Then it races back to the left side of the heart. The next heartbeat sends the life-giving liquid all the way around the body. Because the loop around the body is much longer than the trip to the lungs, the left side of the heart is larger and stronger.

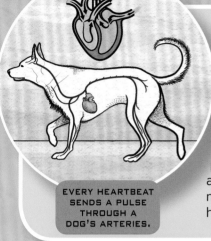

EVERY HEARTBEAT
SENDS A PULSE
THROUGH A
DOG'S ARTERIES.

THE RHYTHM OF LIFE
Lub-dub. Lub-dub. Lub-dub. That's the sound veterinarians expect to hear in a heartbeat. As blood moves from one section of the heart to another, **valves** that separate the sections snap shut. These valves keep the blood from moving the wrong way as the heart squeezes. As the valves slam tight, they create the sounds of the heartbeat.

Each heartbeat sends a surge of blood through the **arteries.** When a large artery runs near the surface of the skin, you can feel that surge as a **pulse.** The best place to feel a dog's pulse is on the inside of one of his back legs. A large artery goes across the top of his leg bone. The heart rate and pulse are about the same if blood is moving smoothly through the body. Occasionally, a dog's pulse is different than the heart rate. The vet knows to check on his blood circulation.

3

TAKE A BREATHER

FIND YOUR DOG'S RESPIRATION RATE

> Difficulty Level:
> **Easy**

> Active Time Needed:
> **5 minutes**

Is your pooch flopped on the floor, lazily eyeing the window? Time for a little spying—all in the name of science. Sneak over, but don't disturb her. Use these steps to figure out her resting **respiration rate,** or how fast she breathes when she's at rest.

YOU NEED

clock or timer
pen and paper or a calculator

INSTRUCTIONS

1 Without disturbing your dog, watch for her ribs to rise and fall.

2 Count the number of times her ribs rise in 15 seconds. If you have difficulty seeing the breaths, try softly laying your hand on her side to feel them.

3 Multiply that number by four to get the number of breaths in a minute. This is her resting respiration rate.

DEEP BREATHS

Your pup's respiration rate (like her heart rate) depends on her size. A massive mastiff may draw a mere 12 breaths per minute, while a tiny teacup poodle takes three times as many. A higher-than-normal respiration rate in a dog that has not been exercising can indicate that she is frightened or in pain. Jot your pup's resting respiration rate somewhere handy. It could be useful for comparison if you are concerned about her breathing in the future. For the present, you can enjoy her smooth breathing by laying your head on her side, matching your breathing to hers, and relaxing together.

NASAL AND SINUS CAVITY

LUNGS

TRACHEA

RUN, ROVER, RUN!

EXPLORE HOW EXERCISE AFFECTS YOUR POOCH

> Difficulty Level:
> **Easy**

> Active Time Needed:
> **30 minutes**

In the previous activities, you found your dog's resting heart rate and respiratory rate. Now it's time to get her moving and see how things change.

YOU NEED

a place to be active
your dog's favorite toys
stethoscope
pencil and paper or
    calculator

POWER UP

Every time your dog moves a muscle, it sets off a whole chain of events:

🐾 The muscle uses energy to contract.
🐾 To make energy, the muscle uses oxygen.
🐾 Then the muscle cells need more oxygen from the blood.
🐾 So the heart beats faster to move the oxygen to the muscles.
🐾 And your dog breathes faster to get more oxygen to the blood.

All of these changes in your dog create heat. So as she exercises, her heart rate increases, her respiration rate goes up, and she gets warm. Whew!

INSTRUCTIONS

1 Before you take your dog on a romp, make a quick check of her temperature using the floppy part of her ear. Gently press your fingers against the underside where there is less hair. Note if it feels warm or cool to you.

2 Get your dog up and moving! Take her for a jog, play an active game of tug, have her chase some balls, or play any game she enjoys. Keep her going for at least 10 minutes.

3 Slide your fingers under her ear and recheck her temperature.

4 Shift to a slower activity until she is calm enough for you to carefully take her post-exercise heart and respiratory rates (using the instructions on pages 35 and 38, respectively).

MUTTS ON THE MOVE

HOW FIDO'S FEET WORK TOGETHER

Difficulty Level:
Medium

Active Time Needed:
15 minutes

Walking is fairly straightforward for a person—you place one foot and then the other. But a dog has four legs to keep sorted. Grab a friend or family member and work together to try all the ways your dog can get going.

YOU NEED

leash
a friend

NO GOING BACK

The muscles on a dog's back end are much bigger than the muscles around his front legs. His front legs are more loosely connected to his spine, so they can serve as shock absorbers as they hit the ground. Dogs hate having to walk backward. They'd rather turn around than have to push with their weak front legs.

TAKE IT FURTHER

Film your dog moving at different speeds. Watch the videos in slow motion for a good look at the pattern of his paws.

INSTRUCTIONS

1 Decide with your friend who will act as the front legs and who will act as the back legs. Line up so the "back legs" are behind the "front legs."

2 Walk forward moving opposite legs. As the front person steps with his left foot, the back person should step with her right. Then the front person should step right and the back person step left.

3 Work together to figure out how many other combinations of footsteps you and your partner can use to walk.

4 Leash your dog and head out for a walk. Watch your dog's legs as he walks. What stepping pattern does he use?

5 Move your dog up to a run. Now what stepping pattern do you see?

SEE HOW THEY RUN

A dog's stepping pattern, or **gait,** depends on the speed that the dog is moving. Not all dogs use all four patterns, and some patterns vary a little between dogs.

Walk: A walking dog moves all four legs at different times. A back leg moves first, followed by the front leg on the same side. The back leg on the opposite side goes next, followed by the other front leg, all in very quick succession. It is like you and your friend using the same legs, with the front person about half a stride behind the back person.

Trot: For most dogs, trotting is their favorite way to run. A trotting dog moves its front leg and the opposite back leg at the same time, or almost at the same time.

Pace: A pacing dog moves both left feet together and then both right feet together. This is the least common gait for most dogs.

Gallop: This is the fastest gait—essentially, a leap from his back to his front legs over and over again. A galloping greyhound can reach 45 miles an hour (72 km/h).

WALK

TROT

PACE

LAP IT UP!
SEE HOW DOGS DRINK

> Difficulty Level:
> **Medium**

> Active Time Needed:
> **20 minutes**

All this exercise can make a dog thirsty! Paws aren't much good for grabbing a glass of water, and dogs can't suck through a straw. They have to use their tongues to quench their thirst. You might think that a dog scoops up water with his tongue. But is that really how it works? A group of researchers decided to find out, and you can try the same experiment yourself.

YOU NEED

bowl of water (clear is best)
camera or phone
video editing software or device with
  slow-motion video capability

INSTRUCTIONS

1 Fill the bowl with water to make it easy to capture your dog's drinking on video.

2 Bring your dog to the bowl. If she is not thirsty, take her for a walk first.

3 Get as close as you can with your camera and film your dog as she drinks. Film her from the side in order to get a clear look of her tongue at work.

4 View the video at the slowest speed available and watch her tongue closely.

TIP
Most computers and phones come with basic video editing software that allows video to be slowed after filming. Many will even let you shoot in slo-mo!

A DOG'S TONGUE MAKES A *J* SHAPE TO GRAB WATER.

GRAB A BITE TO DRINK

At the molecular level, water is sticky. Water molecules are bent, and one side has a slight negative electrical charge. The other side has a slight positive charge. As a result, water molecules cling together—positive end to negative end. They can also stick to other surfaces, such as your dog's tongue.

Researchers at Virginia Tech in Virginia, U.S.A., watched lots of slow-motion video of drinking dogs. They determined that dogs drink by plunging their tongue against the water surface and rapidly pulling it back. When a dog hits his tongue against the water, some of the water molecules stick to the tongue. Other water molecules are stuck to those molecules, and yet other molecules are stuck to that set of molecules and so forth, forming a column all the way down to the bowl. Eventually, the force of gravity pushing down is too strong. The molecules lose their grip on each other and the column collapses.

To get a mouthful of water, dogs bite into the column just before it collapses. They shape their tongue like a *J* to allow a large area from the middle of the tongue to hit the surface, and make a nice, wide column. Gulp!

in the LAB

DOGGIE DONORS

Kayla, a big black Lab, bounds up the steps into the big bus, her tail wagging wildly. She jumps onto the table and lies down. She knows that she loves the treats and attention from the nice people. She doesn't know that she is a hero.

Kayla is one of about 150 dogs who donate blood each year for the Penn Animal Blood Bank in Philadelphia, Pennsylvania, U.S.A. Dogs need donated blood for many of the same reasons that humans do: an accident, an illness, or an emergency trip to the vet. Kayla's blood will give new life to a sick dog.

KAYLA WAITS HER TURN TO GIVE BLOOD.

BLOOD TYPING

Nearby, at the University of Pennsylvania, Urs Giger is studying a blood sample. Giger has been researching animal blood **transfusions** for more than 30 years. He even discovered a new **blood type** in dogs.

A blood transfusion works when the dog that gives the blood and the dog that gets it share the same blood type. If you have ever had blood drawn, the doctor may have told you that your blood was O+ or, perhaps, A-. Human blood can be divided into types A, B, AB, and O. Each type can also be classified as positive or negative. If you get blood from someone with a different type, your immune system may recognize that those blood cells do not belong. It will attack and kill the new blood cells. This is called rejecting the transfusion.

Blood typing for dogs is similar, but the groups are different. Occasionally, a dog will have a matching donor and still reject the blood. Giger studied a Dalmatian who rejected a blood donation. He realized that the dog had a blood type that had never been identified before and named it DAL for Dalmatian. Once he began looking, Giger found DAL in Doberman pinschers and Lhasa apsos as well. Now veterinarians can test for DAL before giving a blood transfusion.

"Our goal is to make blood products as safe for animals as they are for humans," says Giger.

HELPERS HOLD KAYLA TO KEEP HER CALM.

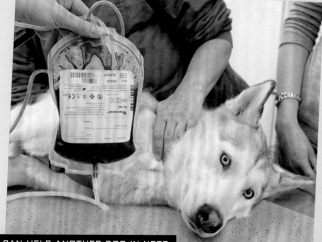

GIVING BLOOD CAN HELP ANOTHER DOG IN NEED.

LAB IN THE LAB

Kayla doesn't seem particularly worried about her blood type and stays calm for the 10-minute blood collection. The Labrador gobbles up her post-donation snack and gives each helper a friendly lick. Then she hops out of the van with a sticker on her head that tells others that she gave blood. Good girl, Kayla!

KAYLA GETS A STICKER AND EATS A TASTY SNACK AFTER DONATING.

Blood donation is not just for dogs! Animal blood banks often collect blood from cats and horses as well.

MAL BLOODMOBILE

THE ANIMAL BLOODMOBILE

School of Veterinary Medicine
UNIVERSITY OF PENNSYLVANIA

Pets Helping Pets

Pets Helping Pets

Greyhounds make especially good blood donors. Many greyhounds are universal donors, which means their blood can be given to any other dog. And their blood has unusually high numbers of red blood cells, which helps recipient dogs recover quickly.

CHAPTER 3

CLEVER CANINES

INSIDE THE MINDS OF DOGS

Ever wish you knew what was going on inside your dog's head? You're not the only one! Ever since humans and dogs began working together, people have been trying to understand how dogs think and learn.

Dogs, on the other hand, are pretty good at understanding people. Say your dog has lost a toy. You point to where it has fallen behind a chair. Your dog heads over to take a look. This may seem like a small thing, but in the animal world, it's huge. Wolves won't follow a point. Chimpanzees walk up and study the end of the human's finger. Only dogs have figured out that pointing sends you toward a target.

Some lucky scientists get to spend their days wrestling (and jumping and digging) with questions about how dogs think. Keep reading and maybe you and your yapper can lick some of these mysteries yourself.

PEEK INTO THE BRAIN

LEFT AND RIGHT SIDES OF THE BRAIN:

Your pooch's thinker is divided into two halves, called hemispheres. The left hemisphere controls the right side of his body, and his right hemisphere controls the left side.

You already know that your dog is an amazing moving and sensing machine. But what controls when he runs and what he sniffs? His brain, of course!

Chaser the border collie is one of the smartest dogs in the world. She knows the names of more than a thousand toys, and she can follow orders that include verbs such as "paw," "nose," or "pick up."

HOW SMART IS YOUR DOG?

It depends on how you define "smart." Just like humans, dogs can be intelligent in different ways. One expert divides dog intelligence three ways. Instinctive intelligence is the skills that come from a dog's breeding. Your collie, for example, may have never seen a sheep, but you'll notice her trying to herd all the people in the house into the same room. Obedience intelligence is how well (and willingly!) a dog learns new commands. Adaptive intelligence is how well a dog solves problems. Dogs can be strong in one area and weak in another. Your dog may not know how to sit or roll over but may be excellent at figuring out how to break into the treat bag!

Picking a dog to learn tricks? Border collies, standard poodles, German shepherds, golden retrievers, and Doberman pinschers learn new commands the fastest.

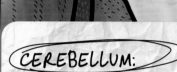

CEREBRUM:

You're saying "Sit!" and your dog is trying to remember what that means he's supposed to do. His cerebrum is hard at work. The cerebrum is the folded, twisty layer that makes the brain look like a plate of spaghetti. It handles learning, memory, and decision-making, and processes information sent in from the sensory organs.

CEREBELLUM:

When your dog is on the move, or even trying to stay in a "sit," it's his cerebellum that is coordinating the messages to and from his muscles to keep them all working together.

Dogs can learn just by watching another dog do something. So if one dog learns how to break into the treat box, better keep an eye on his friends!

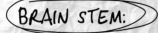

BRAIN STEM:

It's been a busy day, and Fido is fast asleep on the rug. Some parts of his brain may be resting, but his brain stem is still going strong. The brain stem controls the most basic functions, like breathing, heart rate, and swallowing, so it never rests!

A PUZZLE FOR YOUR POOCH

DISCOVER HOW FAST YOUR DOG LEARNS

Your new puppy wants a bit of your pizza. He tries sitting at your feet and whining. No deal. He paws at your knee and gets pushed away. Then he notices that your baby sister dropped some on the floor. Score! Tomorrow night, he'll head straight for the baby's chair. That's learning. You can test your dog's ability to learn by giving him this puzzle and seeing if he can solve it faster with practice.

YOU NEED

9 bite-size treats
3 tennis balls
muffin tin
stopwatch or clock
pencil and paper

INSTRUCTIONS

1 Set three treats into different holes in the muffin tin. Show the muffin tin to your dog to get him interested.

2 Place a tennis ball on top of each treat and set the muffin tin on the floor.

3 Start timing. Record how long it takes your dog to uncover all three treats.

4 Repeat the procedure and record how long it takes him to find all the treats a second time.

5 Give him one more round and record the time for his third attempt.

6 Compare the three times. If your dog was faster on his second and third tries, it shows that he learned how to extract the treats quickly.

SIT. STAY. LEARN!

Whenever a dog does something and gets a reward, he is more likely to do it again. Psychologists call this **conditioning**. The problem is, dogs are in constant motion. It takes a lot of work to teach them which move is being rewarded. You can almost imagine your dog's thoughts the first time you reward him for a trick, "Oh, I wagged my tail. Is that why I got the treat? I sneezed. Did that do it? Maybe she gave me a treat because I wiggled my ears." Gradually, your dog will realize which action earns the treat.

Treat puzzles work similarly. Spot smells the treat and knows it's there. He may try several ways to get it out: nudging with his nose, pushing with his paw, and looking at you to see if you'll get it for him. With enough practice, he'll figure out the best way to get the treat, and soon he'll be gulping them down.

TIP
If the ball sinks all the way into the muffin tin opening, it may be difficult for your dog to move the ball. Try using a muffin tin with slightly narrower openings or a thick treat that will elevate the ball a little.

3

PICK A PAW

TEST YOUR PUP'S PAW PREFERENCE

It's not just people who favor one hand over the other! Dogs can be left-handed, or rather, left-pawed, too. With these three activities, you can find out if your dog is a righty or a lefty.

YOU NEED

treat holder (store-bought or made with the activity on page 53)
painter's tape
treats (store-bought or made with the activity on page 22)

INSTRUCTIONS

1 For the first test, offer your dog the treat holder with a treat in it. Record which paw he uses most to stabilize the treat holder while he works to get the treat out. Repeat with a second treat.

2 For the second test, place a small bit of painter's tape on the end of your dog's nose, right in the center. Record how many times he uses each paw as he removes it.

3 For the third test, find a piece of furniture with a low edge, such as a sofa or a bookshelf. It should be low enough that your dog cannot stick his head under, but with enough room for a paw. Show your dog a treat and then slide it under the furniture. Record how many times he uses each paw to try to reach the treat.

4 Add up how many times your dog used each paw in the tests. Did he favor one paw more often?

RIGHTY OR LEFTY?

About one-third of dogs are right-pawed, one-third are left-pawed, and one-third don't seem to have a preference. So whatever your results, your dog is in good company. Dog (and human!) brains have two sides, called hemispheres. These hemispheres show a strange reversal: Body parts on the right side of the body, such as a dog's right paws, right legs, and right eye, are controlled by the left side of his brain. Body parts on the left side of the body are controlled by the right side of the brain. If your dog favors his right paw, he's using his left hemisphere. If he prefers his left paw, you could say he's in his "right mind."

HIDE-N-GO TREAT

MAKE A TREAT HOLDER

> Difficulty Level:
> **Grab a Grown-up**

> Active Time Needed:
> **5 minutes**

It might seem like your dog has it all. You provide the food, water, and shelter. You take her out when she needs to pee. All your pooch has to do is lie around. While that might seem like a wonderful life, your dog may find it boring. Wild animals are constantly solving problems: looking for new food sources, protecting themselves from predators, and looking for shelter. When you give your pooch puzzles or teach her new tricks, it keeps her thinking and banishes her boredom. Make this treat holder to give her brain *and* her mouth something to chew on.

INSTRUCTIONS

1 Ask your helpful adult to make a three-inch (7.6-cm) cut across the center of the tennis ball, using the utility knife. (If you have a smaller ball, the cut should go about halfway around the ball.)

2 Squeeze the ball and place a treat inside. If your treat is too big to fit in the ball, break it in half. Your dog will have to chew on the ball to get the treat out.

1

2

YOU NEED

a grown-up
utility knife
tennis ball (If you have a very small
     dog, you may need the miniature
     tennis balls sold in pet stores.)
dog treats

CATCH THIS YAWN!

FIND OUT IF YOUR YAWNS ARE CONTAGIOUS

Difficulty Level:
Easy

Active Time Needed:
5 minutes

Have you ever seen a friend yawn, and then found yourself yawning as well? Scientists call this "contagious yawning." Some dogs spread the yawns as well. Does yours?

YOU NEED

a calm pup

INSTRUCTIONS

1 Sit on the floor in front of your dog and get her attention by calling her name.

2 Think about a time you were very, very tired and imagine your best friend yawning. This should give you the urge to yawn. Make eye contact with your dog and let the yawn go. Feel free to make some noise as you do it.

3 Repeat several times, making sure that you have eye contact with your dog each time, and see if your dog follows suit.

OPEN WIDE Don't worry if your dog just stares at your yawning face or dives in for a quick kiss. In one experiment, only about half of the yawned-at dogs yawned back. Yawning is a bit of a mystery. Scientists know that animals yawn when they are tired, bored, or stressed, but it isn't clear how yawning helps in any of those situations. Contagious yawning is even more of a mystery! Some scientists have wondered if it is a form of **empathy,** or understanding how someone feels. They found that when people "catch" a yawn, they use the same parts of the brain that are used in feeling empathy. In humans, children begin to catch yawns around age four, about the same time that they start understanding other children's feelings. Puppies join the contagious yawning club around seven months old. Whatever the cause of the contagion, no other animals have been found to share a yawn across species.

TAKE IT FURTHER
Have different members of your family give yawning a try. In some studies, dogs were more likely to respond to a person they knew well.

RUFF REFLECTION

CAN YOUR DOG RECOGNIZE HERSELF IN THE MIRROR?

> Difficulty Level:
> **Easy**

> Active Time Needed:
> **15 minutes**

If you have a little spaghetti sauce on your chin and catch your reflection in a mirror, you grab a napkin and wipe your face. According to neurobiologists, that little act of cleaning reveals a lot about you. It means that you know that the person in the mirror is you. After all, you wipe your own chin, not the one in the reflection. It also means, at some level, you know that you exist as an individual. Animal researchers call this self-awareness, and they use a mirror test to see if animals have it. Try the traditional mirror test on your dog.

YOU NEED

half-inch (13-mm) square of blue painter's tape

mirror

TIP
Set the tape lightly on her fur so it's easy to remove.

MIRROR, MIRROR

If your dog recognizes herself in the mirror and tries to remove the mark from her own head, she has passed the mirror test and is considered to be self-aware. This would make your dog quite extraordinary! Chimpanzees and orangutans pass the mirror test. Dolphins pass the mirror test. Human babies can usually pass the mirror test by the time they turn two. Dogs, however intelligent they seem, consistently fail the mirror test in research labs. Why?

Perhaps it is because dogs rely on smell more than looks to figure out who's who. After all, a dog's sense of smell is much stronger than her sense of sight. Several researchers are working on smell tests that might replace the mirror test for pups.

1

INSTRUCTIONS

1 Show your dog her reflection in a mirror. Does she react as if she is seeing another dog? Is she more interested in the mirror itself than the reflection?

2 Set the mirror aside. While petting your dog, slip the square of painter's tape onto her forehead, where it will be visible in the mirror but not touching her sensitive whiskers.

3 Allow her to play for a few minutes and see if she seems to notice the tape. If so, reposition it.

4 Show her the mirror again. Does she seem puzzled that her face has a new mark on it? Does she try to remove it?

In the past, dogs couldn't recognize images on TV. To a dog's eye, older televisions appeared to flicker. But that's changed with modern screens. Now, there are even online channels just for dogs!

4

in the LAB

SNIFFING OUT THE POOCH PEE MYSTERY

Take your pup for a walk and he'll start a sniffing frenzy. And it's likely that your dog gets pretty excited when he discovers the neighbor dog's bathroom spot. But his nose might be less enthusiastic when you circle the block and come back to his very own potty spot.

Alexandra Horowitz, from the Dog Cognition Lab at Barnard College in New York City, knew that dogs generally ignore their own urine puddles when they're outside. Instead, they devote their sniffing time to pee from other dogs. As you saw on page 56, dogs don't usually recognize themselves in a mirror. But could it mean that dogs instead use their powerful sense of smell to identify each other—and even themselves? To find out, she has designed a new sort of "mirror test" that would allow dogs to use their sense of smell to show that dogs have self-recognition.

DOGS IN HOROWITZ'S EXPERIMENT INVESTIGATE THE SCENTS.

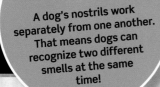

A dog's nostrils work separately from one another. That means dogs can recognize two different smells at the same time!

MAKING HER MARK

In the mirror test, the researcher places a mark on an animal's face when the animal is unaware to see if the animal tries to remove it when he sees it in a mirror. To create an experiment as close to that as possible, but instead using smell, Horowitz decided to try "marking" the dog's urine with an odor that didn't belong, to see if the dogs would spend extra time sniffing and puzzling over the change in their scent. If they spent more time with the marked smell, it could show that they knew themselves well enough to detect a change.

And, eureka! The dogs in her experiment did indeed spend the most time sniffing their own urine with an added odor. Horowitz says this indicates that the dogs recognized themselves and knew something was off. But does this mean dogs really are self-aware? It's still not clear. Animals that pass the mirror test clean off the mark to make themselves look normal again. In Horowitz's study, there is no way for dogs to correct the odd smell. But Horowitz is working to find a solution. Perhaps her research will finally let dogs smell their way to success!

One of the first researchers to study whether or not dogs recognized their own urine got his samples by collecting yellow snow.

CHAPTER 4

PAMPERED POOCHES

USING SCIENCE TO CARE FOR YOUR CANINE

When Spot rolls over and begs for a belly rub, you know you have a happy dog. And when you're having a bad day, nothing beats cuddling with a furry friend. For those good times, you want to keep his fur and skin healthy and soft. How? Science, of course!

In many ways, your dog's skin is similar to your own. You both have a waterproof coating made of dead skin cells. Underneath, you have layers of live skin filled with nerve cells, blood vessels, glands, and follicles that grow hair. And it's pretty obvious that your dog has many more hairs than you do! Each hair is connected to tiny muscles. On a human, those muscles just create goose bumps. For your dog, the muscles can puff his hair to help keep him warm.

Your dog may think a long licking session is all the grooming he needs. Fortunately, you don't have to join in to learn the science behind healthy hair and skin.

SKIN DEEP

Puppies grow soft undercoat hairs. They don't grow rough guard hairs until they are about six months old.

F ido's fur coat starts deep in the layers of his skin. His skin is thinner than yours, and all that hair helps protect it.

HAIR TODAY, GONE TOMORROW

With all that rolling and scratching, your pup's hairs get old and damaged and need to be replaced. Her hair growth moves in a cycle: Each hair grows until it reaches the length predetermined by her **genes.** When it reaches full length, it goes into a resting phase. This happens in winter for many dogs. When spring comes, the growth cycle begins again. The old hairs fall out—and pile up all over the house!

Ranmaru, a labradoodle from Tokyo, holds a world record for the longest eyelashes. His longest lash is 6.69 inches (17 cm) long!

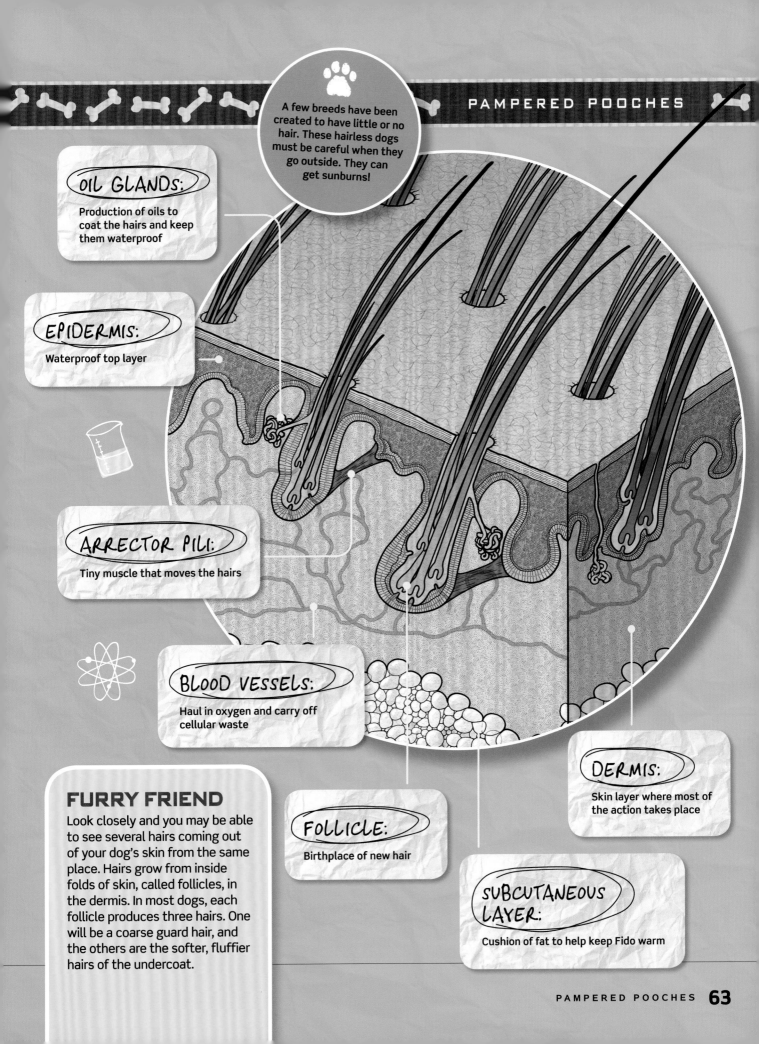

A few breeds have been created to have little or no hair. These hairless dogs must be careful when they go outside. They can get sunburns!

OIL GLANDS:

Production of oils to coat the hairs and keep them waterproof

EPIDERMIS:

Waterproof top layer

ARRECTOR PILI:

Tiny muscle that moves the hairs

BLOOD VESSELS:

Haul in oxygen and carry off cellular waste

DERMIS:

Skin layer where most of the action takes place

FOLLICLE:

Birthplace of new hair

SUBCUTANEOUS LAYER:

Cushion of fat to help keep Fido warm

FURRY FRIEND

Look closely and you may be able to see several hairs coming out of your dog's skin from the same place. Hairs grow from inside folds of skin, called follicles, in the dermis. In most dogs, each follicle produces three hairs. One will be a coarse guard hair, and the others are the softer, fluffier hairs of the undercoat.

COZY CANINES

DISCOVER HOW A COAT KEEPS YOUR DOG WARM

When your dog heads out to do his business on a frosty morning, his fur coat may not be enough to keep him from shivering. You know you can keep him toasty in a dog sweater, but why does adding a sweater turn up the heat? Try this activity to find out how a sweater can take your dog from cool to cozy.

YOU NEED

dog sweater or coat (If you don't have one, see the activity on page 66.)
scientific thermometer
pencil and paper

INSTRUCTIONS

1 Place the thermometer on a table and record the temperature.

2 Put the sweater on top of the thermometer. In 15 minutes, check and record the temperature again.

3 Lay the thermometer on your dog's back. Hold it in place until it stabilizes, but be careful not to have your hand on the bulb of the thermometer. Record the temperature.

4 Put the sweater on your dog and have him wear it for at least 20 minutes.

5 Check your dog's temperature again. This time, slide the thermometer under his sweater to the same place where you checked it earlier. Hold the thermometer in place until the temperature stabilizes—again be careful not to have your hand on the bulb of the thermometer. Record the temperature.

KEEPING COOL

For an animal stuck in a fur coat, summer brings other problems. Dogs have only a few sweat glands, located between their toes. The sweat evaporates off their bare paw-pads and cools them. This is hardly enough to keep a dog cool, so dogs release extra heat anywhere they don't have fur.

Pant ... pant ... pant. You've seen your dog at it. Blood vessels surround the inside of a dog's mouth, and the blood inside them is hot. Dogs pant to draw cool air across those blood vessels, cooling the blood, which cools the body. Grab a flashlight and peek at the inside of his ears. See the fur-free areas? Look for blood vessels that run close to the surface to release heat.

TIP
The kind of thermometer you use when you're sick won't work with this activity. You'll need one that measures a larger range of temperatures.

4

5

KEEPING WARM

A coat can't make heat all by itself, so the thermometer on the table doesn't warm up just because it is under a coat. What a coat can do is *trap* heat. If you pet your pup, you can feel that he is warm. Ordinarily, his body heat radiates into the air around him. Coats and sweaters trap the warm air so the heat isn't carried away. Your dog stays warm.

BUNDLE UP!

MAKE A DAPPER DOG COAT

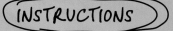

Difficulty Level:
Grab a Grown-up

Active Time Needed:
30 minutes

Dog breeds developed their fur coats to match the temperatures in the places where they were bred. But as people have moved around the world, so have dogs. Your pup may find that her fur is not enough on chilly winter days. Make her a sweater to keep her cozy!

YOU NEED

old sweater or sweatshirt
scissors
tape measure
duct tape or needle and thread

WIDTH ACROSS BACK BETWEEN SHOULDERS

WIDTH BETWEEN FRONT LEGS

LENGTH OF DOG'S BODY

TIP
You may have to look around to find an old sweater or sweatshirt that is the right size. Consider both adult and kids clothes. You can also use duct tape to make the sweater bigger or smaller.

INSTRUCTIONS

1 If you have a small dog, you will make the coat from the sleeve of your old sweater. With an adult, cut along the shoulder seam to remove the sleeve.

If you have a large dog, you will use the body of the shirt. Have an adult help you trim both sleeves off along the shoulder seam. Then sew or tape the armholes shut. If you use duct tape, apply tape to the inside and outside of the shirt. Be sure to firmly press down all of the edges of the tape to ensure there is nothing sticky that would catch your dog's fur.

2 Take three measurements:

a Measure the length of your dog's body from the neck to the base of his tail. Divide this length by two.

b Measure across his back from the top of one front leg to the top of the other.

c Measure the distance between his two legs on his belly.

3 Use those measurements to cut leg holes according to the diagram. If the area around the holes begins to fray, sew or tape the edges.

4 If needed, trim the bottom of the sweater to keep it off of your dog's tail.

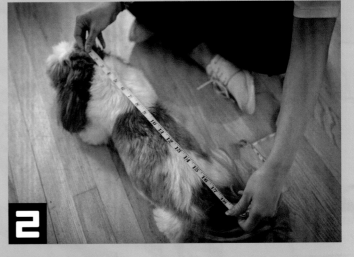

FUR COATS Of course, your dog was born with his very own fur coat. Grab a wad of hair from your dog brush to check it out. If your dog has short fur, gently run your hand over his coat. Several hairs will likely collect on your hands. You'll see two sorts of strands. The long, coarse hairs are called **guard hairs.** These are the hairs that are most obvious when you look at your pooch. For example, if you have a black dog, those hairs will be black. You will also see shorter, fluffy hairs called **secondary hairs.** Secondary hairs may be white, light brown, or gray, even if your dog doesn't look that color. Secondary hair is masterful at trapping warm air. Thick, puffy dogs like shelties, chow chows, and huskies have thick undercoats of secondary hair. They rarely need extra sweaters. Poodles, pugs, and greyhounds have fewer secondary hairs and easily get the shivers.

HALF BATH

FIND OUT IF SHAMPOO IS RIGHT FOR YOUR PUP

> **Difficulty Level:**
> **Grab a Grown-up**

> **Active Time Needed:**
> **20 minutes initially, then 10 minutes a week for 4 weeks**

If you wore a coat all the time, eventually it would have to be washed. What about your furry friend? Experts disagree on how frequently a dog needs washing. Try shampooing just one side of your dog to figure out the ideal washing schedule for your pooch.

YOU NEED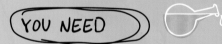

hose or bathtub with cup
    for pouring
shampoo made specifically
    for dogs
towels

TIP
Make sure you pick a shampoo for pooches. A dog's skin is less acidic than human skin, so human shampoo can cause irritation.

1

2

3

4

RATING SCALE

ODOR:
1. PLEASANT AROMA. I'D USE HIM AS A PILLOW.
2. SMELLS LIKE A DOG, BUT NOT IN A BAD WAY.
3. STARTING TO GET A LITTLE STINKY. I WOULDN'T WANT HIM ON MY BED.
4. PEE-EW! THIS DOG REEKS. IT'S A BATH EMERGENCY!

DIRT AND OIL:
1. LOOKS CLEAN AND FEELS SOFT.
2. LOOKS CLEAN, BUT LEAVES A LITTLE ICKY FEELING ON MY HANDS WHEN I PET HIM.
3. DIRT SHOWS IN A FEW PLACES.
4. GOOD GRIEF! DON'T EVEN COME IN THE HOUSE LIKE THAT!

7 In four weeks, analyze your data. If the side without shampoo stayed fresh and clean, or was less likely to need a scratch, rinsing and brushing may be all he needs. On the other hand, if the side with shampoo stayed in better shape, a good soap and scrub may be the way to go.

INSTRUCTIONS

1 Begin by wetting your dog thoroughly. You may need to rub his fur with your fingers to help the water soak in.

2 Decide which side of his body you want to shampoo. To make it fair, pick the left or right side, not the front or back, as dogs do very different things with their hind ends than their front. Remember which side you picked!

3 Pretend there is a line running down the center of your dog's back, from his nose to his tail. Carefully shampoo your dog on the side you selected. Be sure to get his back, legs, paws, and belly on this side. Avoid his head if you aren't sure you can keep the shampoo out of his eyes and ears.

4 Thoroughly rinse the shampoo, so none of it is left to irritate his skin.

5 Towel him dry.

6 Check out his cleanliness over the next four weeks. Twice a week, use the rating scales on this page to evaluate his odor and dirt levels. Jot down which side he scratches each time you observe it.

TAKE IT FURTHER
Try comparing two different shampoos by washing one side with one shampoo and one with the other. Does it matter which brand you buy?

TO BATHE OR NOT TO BATHE
Some dog experts believe that too many baths are bad for a dog's skin. They argue that the oils in his fur are natural and removing them can irritate his skin and make him more likely to stink. Other experts believe that bathing regularly, with the right sort of shampoo, is exactly what a pooch needs to stay clean, healthy, and fresh-smelling. In all likelihood, there is truth in both positions. Some dogs probably keep their coats naturally neat. Others have a knack for finding the nastiest place in the yard to go for a roll.

SUPER SUDS

SEE SHAMPOO AT WORK

Open a bottle of dog shampoo and give it a sniff. There's a sweet, fresh smell. Rub a little shampoo between your fingers. It feels slippery. What's going on with shampoo? How does it transform your filthy Fido into a huggable hound?

YOU NEED

loose dog hair (from your dog's brush)
two bowls
water
dog shampoo

LIKE OIL AND WATER

You have probably noticed before that oil and water don't mix. Your dog's skin releases natural oils to protect his hair and make it water-proof. That's great in a rainstorm, but not at bath time. It's hard to get the water to soak into his fur! This is where the shampoo comes in. Shampoo contains molecules that connect with water on one side and oil on the other. It links the clean water to the dirty oil, allowing the oil to be rinsed away. After the bath, your dog's skin will produce a fresh coat of oil to protect his hair.

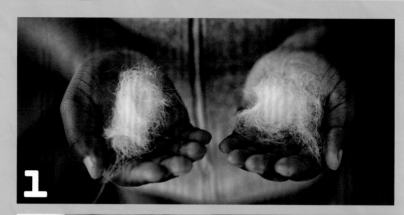

5

TAKE IT FURTHER
Try getting wads of hair dirty in different ways. Rub them in the mud or coat them with vegetable oil. How thoroughly does the dog shampoo clean them? Do different shampoos work differently?

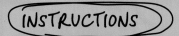

INSTRUCTIONS

1 Rub two clumps of hair between your fingers to make two wads of loose dog hair.

2 Fill the bowls with water.

3 Drop one of the wads into a bowl of water.

4 Put a very small drop of shampoo on the other wad of hair. Rub it in so that it is lightly coated, not drenched in shampoo.

5 Drop the shampooed wad into the other bowl of water and observe.

NOSE PRINT

CAPTURE YOUR DOG'S UNIQUE MARK

Take a look at your dog's nose. It is one of the few places where you can get up close and personal with her skin, without having to peer through a curtain of hair. The skin on your dog's nose is bumpy, and those bumps form a pattern that is as unique as a human fingerprint. Grab a camera and get a good shot of that schnoz to document your dog's most distinguishing feature.

YOU NEED

a camera

1

3

TIP
If your camera has a macro lens or macro setting, you'll get an even more detailed shot!

MAX

INSTRUCTIONS

1 Choose a time when your dog is resting. Hold the camera in front of your dog's face. Give her a few minutes to sniff it and study it.

2 Moving slowly, open the lens cap and direct the camera at your dog's face. If you stay calm and move slowly, your dog is likely to remain resting.

3 Zoom in on your dog's nose and take a picture.

4 If the sound startled her, allow her to settle back down. Repeat until you get a clear shot of her nose.

5 Compare your dog's snout with the other pictures here, for a sense of just how special your dog's nose print is.

MAISY

JUST GROOVY

Each little bump on your dog's nose is called a **plaque.** See how your dog's nose differs in the shapes of his plaques and how they fit together. When you're done comparing, hold on to the picture. If you ever need to prove he is your dog—or that he didn't leave the nose prints at the scene of a crime—you'll be covered!

When your puppy gives you a nuzzle, you expect his nose to be moist. But dogs don't have any glands on their noses. They have to slop spit over their nose with a big, wet tongue. When they lick, saliva runs through the grooves between the plaques. It drags any odors from the tip of his nose down to where he can smell them. The grooves between the plaques make the skin on his nose look thick, but that's deceptive. There are actually fewer layers of skin on a dog's nose, so always treat your pooch's snout with care.

CHLOE

in the LAB

STOP THAT ITCH!

Bella was an itchy dog. When Dr. Cherie Pucheu-Haston first met Bella at the Louisiana State University Veterinary Teaching Hospital, in Baton Rouge, Louisiana, U.S.A., she was so miserable that she didn't want to be touched or held. She didn't want to play or run around. All she wanted to do was scratch.

Could Bella be allergic to something she was eating? Allergies happen when the body's immune system confuses something normal—like food—with an invader like a bacteria or virus. The immune system activates its fighting cells to destroy the invader. Many of these cells live in the skin and cause intense itching.

Pucheu-Haston knew what needed to happen. To find out if Bella had food allergies, she had to go on a bland, carefully planned diet for three months. No treats. No rawhide bones. Not even flavored medicines. If Bella got better, she could gradually try her old foods to figure out which ones were causing the itch. It would be a long, difficult process.

BELLA IS HAPPY TO BE ITCH-FREE!

Puggy the Pekinese kept himself clean with a monster tongue. It was 4.5 inches (11.43 cm) long and almost touched the ground as he ran.

A BETTER WAY

There has to be a better way to help dogs like Bella, and Pucheu-Haston is on the case. She would like to develop a blood test that will quickly and easily identify allergy-causing foods. The first step is to figure out which proteins are most likely to set off a dog's immune system. When Pucheu-Haston explained what she was trying to do, Bella's owners were happy to let Bella help.

In her lab, Pucheu-Haston separates proteins found in common foods. She mixes them with small samples of blood donated by dogs like Bella and then tests to see if antibodies in the blood attack the proteins. Then she sees if the proteins that are attacked by the blood are the same ones that cause problems when the dogs eat the foods they are from. She compares these results to blood drawn from dogs without food allergies and hopefully can develop an initial list of common allergy-causing proteins. "This is an early study," Pucheu-Haston says, "there's a lot more research to be done."

Lots of people are allergic to dogs, but some dogs are allergic to people! Never fear, if your pooch has a human allergy, you don't have to give her up. There are several treatments to keep her allergy free.

BELLA BOUNCES BACK

After three months on a limited diet, Bella was a new dog. She bounded into the exam room, tail wagging and tongue licking. "Her owners said that she was more energetic than she had been in years," remembers Pucheu-Haston. Today, Bella is allergy-free, and thanks to her participation in Pucheu-Haston's research, she's helping other dogs get there, too.

GLOSSARY

ARTERIES: blood vessels that carry blood away from the heart

BLOOD TYPE: a grouping that indicates whether blood from one person will be accepted by another

CONDITIONING: learning to associate an action or event with a reward or punishment

CONE CELLS: cells in the eye that detect color

EMPATHY: understanding how another person or animal feels

GAIT: a pattern of foot placement in movement

GENES: biological information passed from parent to child that determines characteristics of the child

GUARD HAIRS: strong, thick hairs that make up a dog's top coat

HEART RATE: the number of heartbeats in one minute

HERTZ: a unit of measurement for pitch that indicates how many sound vibrations pass by in one second

MOLECULES: groups of atoms that are bound together into clusters

OLFACTORY RECESS: a cavelike region in a dog's nose that can hold odor while the dog continues to breathe in and out

PLAQUE: a distinct, raised area on a dog's nose

PULSE: the heartbeat as felt in an artery

RECEPTOR: a cell or area on a cell that responds to a specific type of molecule

RESPIRATION RATE: the number of breaths taken in one minute

ROD CELLS: cells in the eye that recognize light and movement

SECONDARY HAIRS: smaller, thinner hairs that make up a dog's undercoat

TRANSFUSIONS: taking blood from one person or animal and injecting it into another

VALVES: flaps of tissue that open and close to control the movement of blood in the heart

VIBRISSAE: long, stiff hairs that provide a dog with information via touch

VOMERONASAL ORGAN: a special section of the nose devoted to smelling pheromones

DISCOVER MORE ABOUT DOGS

Want to find out more about dogs and science? Grab a parent and explore these other awesome resources to learn more!

BOOKS ABOUT DOGS

Baines, Becky. *Everything Dogs: All the Canine Facts, Photos, and Fun You Can Get Your Paws On!* National Geographic Kids, 2012.

Horowitz, Alexandra. *Inside of a Dog: What Dogs See, Smell, and Know.* Young Reader's Edition. Simon and Schuster, 2017.

Newman, Aline Alexander, and Gary Weitzman. *How to Speak Dog: A Guide to Decoding Dog Language.* National Geographic Kids, 2013.

MORE SCIENCE EXPERIMENTS FROM NATIONAL GEOGRAPHIC

Wheeler-Toppen, Jodi, and Carol Tennant. *Edible Science: Experiments You Can Eat.* National Geographic Kids, 2015.

Young, Karen Romano. *Try This! 50 Fun Experiments for the Mad Scientist in You.* National Geographic Kids, 2014.

Young, Karen Romano. *Try This! Extreme: 50 Fun and Safe Experiments for the Mad Scientist in You.* National Geographic Kids, 2017.

WEBSITES

National Geographic Kids
Visit the Pet Central portal to play games, take quizzes, read awesome articles, and learn fantastic facts about pets of all shapes and sizes!
natgeokids.com/pets

CANINE CORNER

A psychologist and world-renowned canine scientist and behaviorist maintains this blog all about humans' best friends.
psychologytoday.com/blog/canine-corner

DOG SCIENCE GROUP

This website helps connect dog owners with dog citizen science projects in the United States, United Kingdom, and around the world.
dogsciencegroup.org

INDEX

All photos by Matthew Rakola unless otherwise noted: Andrew Brookes/Cultura RF/Getty Images: cover (background); Lori Epstein: 17, 18, 21, 48, 54, 64; Greg Berns/Emory University: 28-29 (all); Csanad Kiss/Shutterstock: 32; Heather Buzby: 44-45 (all); dpa picture alliance/Alamy Stock Photo: 45; Thinkstock/Stockbyte/Getty Images: 58-59 (CTR); Alexandra Horowitz: 58 (UP LE), 59 (images from experiment); Cherie M. Pucheu-Haston: 74, 75; Stuart Armstrong: 18, 25, 26, 36, 38, 48-49, 63, 66

CREDITS

For Mom, Dad, and Jon; my "puppies" Natalie and Zachary; and Calvin, who was always a good dog.
—J.W.T.

Since 1888, the National Geographic Society has
funded more than 12,000 research, exploration, and
preservation projects around the world. The Society
receives funds from National Geographic Partners, LLC,
funded in part by your purchase. A portion of the
proceeds from this book supports this vital work.
To learn more, visit natgeo.com/info.

For more information, visit nationalgeographic.com,
call 1-800-647-5463, or write to the following address:
National Geographic Partners
1145 17th Street N.W.
Washington, D.C. 20036-4688 U.S.A.

Visit us online at nationalgeographic.com/books

For librarians and teachers: ngchildrensbooks.org

More for kids from National Geographic: natgeokids.com

For information about special discounts for bulk purchases,
please contact National Geographic Books Special Sales:
specialsales@natgeo.com

For rights or permissions inquiries, please contact
National Geographic Books Subsidiary Rights:
bookrights@natgeo.com

Designed by Carol Farrar Norton

Library of Congress Cataloging-in-Publication Data

Names: Wheeler-Toppen, Jodi, author.
Title: Dog science / by Jodi Wheeler-Toppen.
Description: Washington, DC : National Geographic Kids,
  2018. | Audience: Age 9-12. | Audience: Grade 4 to 6. |
  Includes index.
Identifiers: LCCN 2017050021| ISBN 9781426331534
  (paperback) | ISBN 9781426331541 (hardcover)
Subjects: LCSH: Dogs--Juvenile literature. | Dogs--Behavior--
  Juvenile literature.
Classification: LCC SF426.5 .W48 2018 |
  DDC 636.7/089689142--dc23
LC record available at https://lccn.loc.gov/2017050021

The publisher would like to thank the following people
for making this book possible: Kate Hale, senior editor;
Brett Challos, senior designer; Lori Epstein, director of
photography; Paige Towler, associate editor; Sanjida
Rashid, associate designer; Anne LeongSon and Gus Tello,
production designers; Molly Reid, production editor; and
Jennifer Kelly Geddes, fact checker. Special thanks also to
Hilary Andrews, Sarah Mock, Christina Ascani, and Sanjida
Rashid for their assistance on the various photo shoots.
The team is also especially grateful to the Absher-Schantz
and Smith families for kindly allowing the team to take over
their homes while photographing this book.

Printed in China
18/RRDH/1

THE AUTHOR WOULD LIKE TO THANK
Gregory Berns, Peter Cook, Brenda DuVal, Urs Giger,
Danielle Holt, Alexandra Horowitz, Kimberly
Marryott, Sean Owens, Cherie Pucheu-Haston, and
Traci Gunter Williams for generously sharing their
time and expertise in interviews for this book.

She is also thankful for Banjo, Daisy, Elijay, Emmie,
Ivy, Pepper, Piper, Rosie, Roxy, Willie, and Zorro for
helping develop the activities in this book.